I0756255

FINISHING LINE PRESS
www.finishinglinepress.com

MAKING FIGURES IN THE WARD

poems by

George Seli

Finishing Line Press
Georgetown, Kentucky

MAKING FIGURES IN THE WARD

ISBN 979-8-89990-489-9 First Edition

ACKNOWLEDGMENTS

Afternoon Anson (*Epicenter*, 2007)
Apt. 27 (*Kaleidotrope*, 2011)
Astoria in December (*Blue Unicorn*, 2020)
Boy Enigma (*Argestes*, 2007)
Breakfast Men (*Crab Creek Review*, 2009)
Making Figures in the Ward (*The Conium Review*, 2013)
Pastward Shadows (*The Big Windows Review*, 2024)
Periscoping in Midtown (*FutureCycle Poetry*, 2009)
Ranch House (*Freshwater*, 2006)
Sleep (*Jasper's Folly*, 2024)
Subterranean School (*Acappella Zoo*, 2009)
Waiters (*Indefinite Space*, 2020)
You, Youth (*Jasper's Folly*, 2024)

Publisher: Leah Huete de Maines
Editor: Christen Kincaid
Cover Art: Van Gogh's *Corridor in the Asylum* (1889): public domain
Author Photo: Maria Aziez
Cover Design: Elizabeth Maines McCleavy

Order online: www.finishinglinepress.com
also available on amazon.com

Author inquiries and mail orders:
Finishing Line Press
PO Box 1626
Georgetown, Kentucky 40324
USA

Contents

AFTERNOON ANSON

a
candle quietly
in the
mandolin house

where he wavers, oh my
like a note or a flame.

and there's nothing more depressing
than Anson spreading
marmalade alone

except

the remembered sound
of his wife in a frock
of ghostly white
driving away in that yellow,
now outdated car.
"Serenade" it was called.

yes, its motor's
faint staccato
is the one he can't fight
blasting FM static or scraping
burnt toast.

in the bedroom it's made him
a cottony fool
performing nightly,
tossing and turning in time
with his past.

alas. putter away, Anson

to the rosebushes.
each flower wears a clip-on butterfly
and dutifully awaits your snip.
drift by them in a sweater
with a silver V-neck, rather like
open shears.

BREAKFAST MEN

Morning came in a dishabille of ragged clouds.
Ruddy kids barreled across the lawn.
They played or were part of some greater
game. Stark rustling newspapers
interrupted my calm,
along with buzzing wasps.
Frail brown wizards with boggled bodies
affixing an empire by the window.

A sign stood down the road: BEER MILK.
These white monolithic letters
outstripped the shelf life
of any possible hope.

We knew this. We were outstretched, hapless
on the parched sofa landscape.
My brother's large blanched arms
held no woman…
But perhaps a dove
fluttered near his roof antenna
in pursed flight.

Might its buttery wings point west?
Might a sudden sunbeam poke through the blinds?
In this tired pantomime of breakfast,
we'd have rushed out at the sign
of the slightest prophecy.

Living-room air suspended crystal moistures
like grape jelly, smooth as somberness.
Beyond the pane spread
a wide blue sky but my eye
was caught within a small black square
of burnt toast.

RANCH HOUSE

Evening will be smuggled into the house like coals
by imps with little, inhuman faces—
our murky relatives, hardened by old arguments.
They have quick, incendiary tongues.
They move in swiftly, unavoidably.
I know when to step out.

Outside there is unyielding dirt and a horizon
drawn around me like tough leather.
I look ahead at my brother.
He is short in a black jacket, still as
an iron spike driven into the ground.
He has been suddenly inundated by
the brown heaviness of the shed
while standing by it.
We know to say nothing of nothing
of wit or weather.

Is it just skittles going on at home?
After all, it's that "game" of life.
Perhaps a glass racketeer has slipped
on battery acid on the porch where
the teary spinster moved herself
and then resigned. I try not to understand
these games or rules.

Oh, I've read the manual. Granddaddy wrote it.
But now he's stored by his antique rifle collection.
His great hair is mussy, his one good eye squints
as if he's aiming—it works well enough,
just well enough, to see the point
of still living. (His shadow will chill
spring's first flowers.)

His good booklet ain't quite the Bible, of course.
But it told me exactly what to expect, like right now
that Uncle Dack's lathering himself with the last
light of day—and leaving none for his children.

Years later, he'll stumble drunk into
his daughter's abandoned room, alarmed
by the Dairy Ghost. The few animals he
once painted on her wall will distance
themselves from him. They'll seem mangy,
unrecognizable, near death—the red
paint of their innards—on his hands.

Speaking of paint, my brother's an artist,
you know. He feels in color.
The last thing he painted
was with a small, discarded brush—
"wish wish" went its quick strokes over
a fallow canvas, then—
brash auburn, everywhere.
Struggling against the frame,
it could grow nowhere else.

We hung it in the living room, near the circle of beaten couches
we sink into on a Sunday, facing each other weakly,
a tarantula of mist and gloom perched lightly
with a leg on each of our hearts.

A snapshot would capture us: skeletons irrigated
by Michelob. A snapshot speaks more than we do.

Here, in this diseased rest, I will
gain less and less
wisdom. I guess
I'd rather hold out for a word
from the lone horse. So I set a chair out on
grassy forever, where it grazes.
Its waving mane signals me to stay.
It has the fierce answer
to life's harshness.
Here it comes.
Wait—that was
the gross sound of it
clearing its throat.
(It's no easy answer.)

PERISCOPING IN MIDTOWN

Reflections of prewar buildings
quiver in my coffee.
People in gray slacks, straight as shears,
advance at a quick clip.
Weeds disappear from memorials,
for even death gets old.
Bushes take whimsical shapes
in the park where tourists eat crepes.

A girl strolls by with
a holiday-red bag. Gusts
ruffle its cold multitude
of sequins like feathers.

It carries little more
than mixed tapes and combs.
New songs and hairstyles,
bold as squawks.
The way it is slung matches
the slant of the rain
across an office tower's
mirror-grid.

Those who understand
fashion and weather are
everywhere, everywhere
everywhere above us,
reclined behind windows.

Those who wonder sprout
unnoticed toward the sun,
their taut faces
squinting at everything.

I sit and sip quietly, varied perspectives
cast upon me. I feel them no more
than points and edges
of angular shadows.

Who knows? Maybe the next gust
will extend my red scarf over me
like an acute accent indicating
I am to be stressed.

ASTORIA IN DECEMBER

to continue soundless in the afterhours
the way flowers fit
into darkness.
sitting bent
on a patio bench.
whirl of ice,
a world
at my expense.
sitting
below
a laughing, long-chinned winter.

the elevated track

awaits the fleece-headed engineer,
awaits the train that keeps adding cars,
the distended cage, articulating in the hail.

commuters sit with silent, jostled faces.
soon the whole—its lights, sound and steel—fits into the darkness
of a neighborhood I do not know.

continuance is the folded, unopened bills
in my coat pocket. their crisp numerical black

will spread across the kitchen table. I head inside.

TENEMENT

tomato sauce bubbles.
crystal beads dangle above

a girl, Miranda, on satin sheets.
the phone delicately appends
to her face with a red double pucker.
her room is vaulted under leagues of smog …

a tenement
of unknown men,
their noses
jutting from windows
of polyhedral complexity,
their silhouettes fanning out
in the hallways
like playing cards:

must she choose one?

this place of perfidy
is ghosted with unpaid debts.
a cobwebbed radiator
stands quiet as a mausoleum

in the corner.
soap traces
frame a rusty cubism
of old razors.

eventually
blood bubbles
and boils in the breasts
of the unchosen.

that saucy girl …
so standoffish.

a creaking iteration
of floors
rises into the sky,

and time
is honeycombed with veterans
and children
playing with
radios and Oreos.

HOWLING AND THE SHUTTERED HOME

let not these harsh winds touch
the growth of thought

behind boarded-up brows
worn and worried by winter.

two friends in green wingback chairs wonder,
in the teapot's great shadow:

might this world contain something
undiscovered, bat-like,
an Empath?

the garden manages a man-shaped tendril
that extends over the doorstep.

but this feral leaf-man is soon blown away.

the long street is like a tunnel of endless ciphers:
coats and closures
in cold succession.

back in the garden
the rusted lantern swings
like a frail arm
casting about for its glow.

the season's dark mesh falls over the tea sippers.
hope becomes interstitial.
it might be glimpsed in the spiral-patterned teacups
as they are being washed.

spiraling upward or downward?
let's imagine upward, my friend,
though the wind
is orthogonal to our thought.

the den is merely a place to sit,
green, curved and winged.

to fail to hear
an abyss being quietly knitted.

LIGHTNING AND LEAVES

the leaves
move
   shift
over me
  like dark
spastic hands.

a twinge,
  twig,
a thin
snapped light
is the vic-
  tim.

deep
in a gorge
another
moonbeam
has fallen—
an irretrievable baton.

lightning exposes
the skeletal truss
of a cabin, whose slanting roof
chops a place for me
in this neck
of the woods.

Morning revisits
the world infirm,

stepping over blasted pine

wearing timorous orange …

Another baton of light is tossed
quietly over the trees—
my rigid eye in the cabin window sees it.
I'm the stone in the creek's throat,
a curse riffling the leaves.

Lightning was once,
lightning at last, on this trunk
is a cindered hand, a lost grip
on the earth.

No spark is reclaimed
among trees past and present,
a rolling landscape
blurring into the thousands…
So my dream goes.
But the rhododendron
the rhododendron stays,
coaxed long ago
from violence to violet.

And with it, wilted,
is what turned
crackling, cackling brown
underfoot.

Who is dispensed with
in the brush?

A writhen branch,
an unnatural part of nature—

no one will come across
its petrified threat
against the sky.

SLEEP

bronze accents
on double doors
cast signals of morning.

gardenias and spaces
where dreams could be.

lions lunge forth
in spirited stone.

humidity a phantasm
around patio daybeds.

long-hanging kumquats,
scorching ripe.

waiting for a paramour—
has an architecture.
the waiting has been whitewashed.

the wanting is flaking, the aching
is sun baked. the wanting
has turned to sleep.

a plush patterned palm forgettance.

APT. 27

In smoky apprehension,
I hear the twist of invertebrates in the pot.
My hand struggles for things in my pocket,
like a gypsy in the back of a caravan. Odds and ends
beaten into being from the shadows of the kitchen
fade into nebulous cabinets and drawers.
Only the moon had been crisp. Exact.
It'd hung in the window like an Arcadian lamp.
The tongue on the grill speaks in simmers,
slurs of animality. And I sit and wonder whether
the dried husk of calamity is edible. Whether the bits
of life that can be seized are intelligible.
Can one make a stock from bare essentials,
a broth from near-naught?
The moon had been clear, but far from Apt. 27.
It might as well have been a bent silver coin.
The landlord rushes in—

stumbling with a heavy yellow flashlight.
That was it! The Golden Rod of Truth.

"What's going on in here?"
"Have you lost contact with banality?"

He fixes my breaker box and looks disdainfully
at my supper, torn steaming off the bone.
I flash my teeth, each
ignobly crowned.

COAT & LAGER

That murky feeling in a bar
of not knowing, among wood and shadows,
what never fails to bring us down.
It's no blunderbuss of newsprint,
no arthritic tolling of a bell
out in the cold. Not the coven
of bureaucrats, crimson scrawls
in papery dens. Perhaps it's in this very

glass, holding a draught
ready to be lobbed
into a throat that feels

bottomless, with wet walls.
Perhaps, in esophageal corridors,
intestinal tracts or further below,
in deep earth …
lies the shell of a great mood stabilizer,
a pitted counterweight,
an iron winch. Archimedes used it
to raise a bronze sun
for just one man, lever his chin
against tides of disease, tides of war.

Where is it?
Where is that old system
of pulleys and stones?

You—whose gaze has fallen
to the wooden floor—don't know. Bits of dirty ice
are foothills of a looming walk back home,
where lamps have long
been turned off.

You'll rise from that upholstered cocoon
swinging a briefcase in the brightness—
its shadow quick as a moth—
living from the momentum.

OCEANUS

Oceanus is
    a malaise in gentle waves …
    lapping beneath
    a callous crown of pincers.

Oceanus presides
    in salt, light, cigarette haze

& an orange-roofed Howard Johnson
is a washout of time …

gaggles of children, ashy placemats.

Oceanus rules
    over the shells of persons,
    medicated legions of
    seaside citizens

& the convertible
zipping past the condominiums
  is an
  aquamarine disaster

(carrying, as it does,
shopping bags whirling in a tempest
of a relationship).

Oceanus blew
        our days forward in bright, steel-beamed
        rotating capsules
        with shoreline views …
        but now

Oceanus is
   a dull roar
   & a runaway darkness

that swallows
lone woman on a balcony, grizzled man
angling a cue stick.

Oceanus is laissez-faire
as to the waves
            laissez-faire
as to the ocean,

& the choppy goodbyes
shifting us this way and that …

WAITERS

the rooftops of Mulberry Street
cut the sky into a chasm,
a fall zone of stark blue.

heavy shadows
silently forklifted into place
beside dumpsters.

red brick walls
topped with white smoke,
the chasm's busy edges.

the reverse fall
falling away
from booksy banters and day jobs,
the goings-on,
windup goings-on of Mulberry Street.

escape upward, impossibly,
like that Key Food bag
free of the weight of sustenance,
infused with chaotic air,
translucent (still dirty),

a spirited plastic bird.

or—take building blocks
as offices and wait, patiently,
to be verticalized?

pendulous heads
think from side to side.

FOG OVER PLINTHS

far overhead
flew the Abstruse
after pecking about
on 1-dimensional legs.

some of its esoteric plumage
remains on the sand.

the copita used as a loupe
one evening
lies discarded.
the subtle veritas it revealed
forgotten
and sand
blows daily into the bulb.

what shall we uphold?
shoulders and stones
wait to uphold.

great pilings rise
near the shore.
a dwelling, a life pining
to find itself is
cantilevered over rushing water.

ancient questions dissolve.
the Abstruse is extinct.
its feathers are curiosities.
question marks, like pieces of coral,
are reclaimed by the sea,
the primordial swirl.

the plinths are always there
in the swirl.
the plinths make us think.

A SMALL ROUND CONTAINER

febrile grass
sedated by wind
a large man sleeping
in a white shirt
the sun
caverning
with its breath.

waiting with whiteout
for pain care & wonder.

waiting with whiteout,
Marlboro capped & flannelled,
loitering

in hot yards, in strip mall
furniture stores

warm wicker
breathes,
heaves
in a morning
of shade that creaks
as it recedes.

even the shade
from a single cloud
is too much to bear,
even for a large man,
barely stirring.

the slightest brush
wet with destruction.

merest brush tip
pointed at sparking wires of possibility
whipping out across the lawn.

a whiteout
that de-creates.
a whiteout of without.

OR NOT TO BE

the open mouth of the garage
is a warm clearing of thought,
circumscribed sky
with hard edges—
the yellow sun
cereal-box bright—
the primordial orb's
blurriness
makes ideas
indistinct.
I open a warm beer
with a crack sudden—
almost tectonic—amid
cement and gravel,
resting my legs on an inner tube.

to be lackadaisical in this ancient light.

or not to be.
a darkness raftered by roots / granules after incineration.

be ↔ not be
a toggle switch of bright chrome
towers unseen
casts a shadowy feeling
over Florida shantytowns.

MATCHBREAKING

Matchmen, matchwomen,
burnt many times—discard themselves
in the snow,
scattered, half-interred,
screaming at each other in
wine-like darkness.

Streetlights coalesce
into the windy semblance
of a candelabra …
"That's wild, so wild…"
she said. "What
are the chances?"

Down the icy road
I know
there's a box
I can slide into
with my fellows,
a bar. A slipcase
for the embers of that evening,
puzzle pieces I'll pull out,
try to solve, fail.
They disintegrate a little more
each day. What did she say, why that mouth
an open flame? It was a risky exchange.

Myriad hotheads in suits and gowns
light the hillsides. Their smoldered trails
show evidence of crisscrossing,
along with the caravans
of rose peddlers and fortunetellers.

How do they retrace
their skid marks
to meet us again and again
at these worn junctures? O,
to lob a rosebud into a firestorm
or the singed lands between us,
their chances are excellent.

SOLSTICE IN THE UNDERPASS

the dance has elapsed
but the threshold has taken hold.
we cannot leave
the era of the ballroom.

our masques lament
boreal desolation,
a village no longer
as the stories told.

we step into
zealous winters
of spidery carriages.

mendacious dark
in a children's park
suffuses
the ice-lined geometry of the blade.

an ingathering
of those with torn mittens,
bare knuckles,

shoes interred in snow.

a bottled sunrise
of aseptic orange
rolls away…

still, there is
solstice in the underpass,
marked by a waltz
of beggarly hands.

DRAFTSMAN

Compasses pirouetted in his dreams.
He feared their elegance
and unerring steel.
The evil for which
he might pencil-in a place,
the victims he might
circumscribe with their lead …

Smart electric ideas
like golden cupolas
fastened themselves to his
neurons during sleep.
Near his bedpost
placid as an empty town square,
a sheet of graph paper
lay on his desk.

Silent droves of pedestrians,
waited to work and worry incessantly
in new buildings. They crowded like
ghosts around his bushy head.

An abandoned wife
tried to hoarsely scream
through the thin-lined geometry
of hallways just conceived.

He awoke at 9 a.m. and lengthened
the living room of Apt. 4B, protracting
the solitary space for Mr. John Clear, tenant to be.
Then he drew the wall that would be stared at
in vicious premeditation.

Still, an Indian rug, a coat rack
and a secret conversation
were scattered somewhere in the future,
without a foyer. Zoning laws vied with floor plans—
the abstract discord meant there was no place
for a muddy boot. This may be just as well.

His eyes, telescoped and draconian,
saw rows of aluminum streetlamps
radiating from the city.
He surveyed it from his window:
a leaden bud dense with danger,
rolling in the winds
of the Eastern Seaboard.

DURWARD ST.

I aim to / I end up
I aim to / I end up
End up living on a derelict row,
A drifting slice
Of the universe.

High / low windows
Brick facades
Roofs underscoring
white smoke
white clouds
white phantoms.

Somewhere in the swirl of rooms
A man smokes, seated at a bare table.
A grandfather's head, clouded with age.
A dreaming child, transfixed by his dead mother.

I get up
Step / teeter
Step / teeter
Teeter toward an empty glass, turn around:
The gin bottle is elegant
but with the iciness of a jailor.

This is / isn't
This is / isn't
This is a garroting of space in life
'til that space lies still
And planting there
An old chair.

From there, into the late hours,
I look across the street to another
Black-windowed wall.
Lasting / expired
Lasting / expired
Lasting candles near the sleepless shellshocked.
Injured stars, dark
Contusions

In a universe that rolls over, unbothered.

ABANDONMENTS

Abandonments
in the district where I live are
permanent. Beside a tenement,
atop an abutment, jacketed shapes
hook onto payphone receivers,
flapping in the wind, shadowed
by their obscurity, listening…

"Just let me see you again. Give me
another chance. You deserve the best…"
The words enter their mouths like sweet bait.
They bite, helpless as pikes on frozen drifts.
Reeled in, they're soon discarded.

Long-dead patrons of the boarded-up
Aquila Theater across the street
had seen acts like that before. Raindrops
tap boards like their fingertips,
impatiently awaiting impresarios
to marionette, boldly marionette the air
with symbols of our relationships:
equalities on strings, estranged
centrifugal dancers, feigning bulls.

It's an easy, corrugated silence
for a golden ápice yeller, with flurry cap
and aria cape, to declare abiding love—
to bring down from the stage
a bouquet of flourishes. Ensconced
in shadow, to face refusal with soliloquy,
to have his gestures wilt.

Finales continue outside,
awkward and unrehearsed.
They never end.

SOLITAIRE

a one and wistful antique shop,
light snow embroidering the pane,
densely shelved
closing-time darkness.

a single star, minted long ago,
silver coin-like
in a black velour slot—
an infinite sky-sided case.

rare finds, everywhere.
rare finds shiver
on branches, rare finds trapped
in a frozen lake.

infiltrated wind
like Hoyle's ghost
shuffling letters
and ledgers.

porch of etched wood,
green storefront,
illumined posts and sills—
an acropolis of the moon.

the icicles.

the icicles are the beards of those
who remember obsolete forms of solitaire.
the icicles will be gone by morning.

the icicles had the glare of monocles.

they pointed to spots on the ground.
they pointed out things. their points will be missed.

the summery lotus. the American lotus
is now the focus
of our attention
outside the antique shop.

CREAM AND IVORY

the front of the house is whitewashed and vaguely Colonial.
the willows' darkly green,
wand-like branches
wield a mist over the time of day.
elevenses or, perhaps, teatime?

Jean's room, a cocoon finely upholstered.
her day tiered with powdered sweets.
Mom's out.

Jeannie,
a cherub in terrycloth
toying with brass faucets.

in the world of a red cushion
an elephant peers from an embroidered window.

in a bay window across the lush lawn
Mr. Oliphant misses his wife.

his appearance
now, and again, and once more at dusk
is haunting and metered.

dusk falls over silence
like the fallboard of a piano.

Jean's on to something creamy,
a puff with red jelly. Mom's back

so soon?

YOU, YOUTH

sparklewet trees
white storefronts

your meandering is but a mist,

ice cream a minaret.

the later light is
a fallen silver.
an old opulence.

peering around columnar rain—
the satyr

a figure cut awkwardly out of
pale pink construction paper

pushed into the darkening scene

of middle-aged couples
estranged in their finery.

few notice the figure

pushed into the scene
by a child.

back to your cone
and sugary citadel.

a pink that is Parisian
perfectly fitted,
a mink-like night
that smothers heartache.

these things remain
in the stores
(in store)

as you are driven off.

BOY ENIGMA

I.

I am a mere stone's fall
from grace.
Autumn won't absolve me.
I have time to ruminate
over my misbeing.
My name is a misprint
the world's not seeing.
I'm inscribed in a house.

The gable is a circumflex
over my head.
I'm difficult to pronounce.

The gable where one
knows no one
knows one.

II.

The rain is a quiet relic.
A sandy-haired girl is yelling.
The sunbeams are a mess of
toy lightsabers in the yard.
Dad's briefcase is imposing
leather. It stands like a dark portal
to somewhere narrow—
and oppressive, perhaps
tomorrow.

Daylight stretches
barely, tightly
over the waiting winter,
like shrink-wrap.
A notice is penned
on a white drift.

The delivery, I expect
is a handcrafted naught.
Everyone had a hand in it.

III.

To begonias, carports, fields,
cavernous afternoons—
we add a teaspoon of meaning,
and watch it dissipate
in the wind or a rake. The crack
of an opened beer interrupts
no thought. Uncles sit and puff.

Understanding is such a
cumbersome tool,
its flat head stuck in cold dirt.
It looks bent and inept.
I don't feel so bad
being misunderstood.

HOW A TEENAGER BLOTS

I expect nothing, remember less.
Between these 2 posts
my hammock is the slow
curvature of space. Above the parking lot
is an erasure. It never rises, never sets,
filled by puffs from a borrowed cigarette,
fed by sips from a stolen can. Yes,

I'll take the colors from the video arcade,
the shimmering characters. I'll try to play
pin-up, patch-up and Ah:
a world for this afternoon.
It fizzles, sure, it fades.
It has a closing time.

It seems to me
things are similar up north.
A girl eyes the familiar
from a glass door
with a certain blankness,
and uncertainty. People exit,
jackets graze each other,
thought littered with ellipses …

That's when I ask myself:
do I really know the life that leaves
just a sylph of a waitress
among coat hooks, trains
and brickyards?

I don't expect to answer that question,
or remember asking it.

SUBTERRANEAN SCHOOL

"I'm still kind of green at this,"
I say as I stumble in sneakers
through tunnels lined with lockers
of grayish ore—a dull beetle,
stumped by rock.

Suddenly I turn *right*. I turn *correct*
and am struck by the crystalline light of the classroom.
Here webbed wings of whispers
                                        bat
unheard about a professor's head,
oblong and smooth—
stratified with knowledge.

Here I must sit until I learn
the equation that is the echo,
its infinite variations—
crumple my complaints in dusty fists
as lessons project overhead
in filmy hieroglyphs.

Here I share the dream of getting high
upon a measureless green
carried by whims
and winds that defy the gravity of theory.

A dean like a djinn will say,
"Let us take a moment
to look down at our shadows
and remember how we were."
Mortar boards fly like felty birds,
testing air.

There is nothing opaque there,
nothing hard or heavy—
"None of the below."

The answer drips singularly
from many dark cranial roofs
peculiarly formed in rows.

PASTWARD SHADOWS

simmering shadows
on a Saturday afternoon
can't be expunged
from city corners
where couples
once met.

couples, now decoupled.

they were only softly joined
like cards in a pyramid.

couples, now decoupled.

it happens inaudibly
throughout the city
like children unstacking blocks.

twinned shadows cast
from distant apartments
finally
touch in cafes and park benches.

their edges vibrate with emotion.
they affect no one and nothing
in those places.

only the casters know
the darkness with which they drape,
the shapes of their absences.

two specters at tea,
silhouettes of what used to be,
are slots that young hopefuls
step into
on a Saturday afternoon.

MAKING FIGURES IN THE WARD

One cranes his neck
above his numbered state to see
a long line of prefigured men
inscribed on the whiteness of life—
sheets, pillowcases, and hallways—
with fading ink.

Their movements are timid estimates.
Their current positions are constants:
Limbs raised lowered stretched bent—
semaphore for incremental pain,
guiding in needle-thin jets
carrying Morpheus' visionaries.
An open-mouth cipher signals
breath encroached by null.

While some bodies convalesce,
others are leaning dance partners
with decay. And eyesight lasts
upon an aluminum medicine tray
until it's taken away
by little steps stuffed with carpet—
mysterious, like the steps to recovery.
Is that where one

Heads, lost to a realm of cotton fibrils,
dreamy inertia? Here, climate-controlled winds
never bend stiff reeds of gauze or undo
a baby-blue bib, but outlast a lord who
blew out something softly consonant with his fate.
Some protector.

Occasionally, faces poke through the curtain
at the realm's edge. Barely recognized,
they'll ask if one remembers A, B, C,
if one realizes the importance of X, Y, Z,
if the fingers raised are 1, 2, 3...?

To have weak smiles and
no answers.

To have one's last moments
mottled by spots of light
puppeted by a familiar unknown.

George Seli is an editor and adjunct associate professor of philosophy, specializing in philosophy of mind and metaphysics. He has written poetry for most of his life and has studied under two notable poets: Susan Mitchell at Florida Atlantic University and Campbell McGrath at Florida International University. Over the last twenty years, his poetry has appeared in a variety of journals including *The Conium Review, Seems, Epicenter, Crab Creek Review*, and *Indefinite Space*. He is influenced by poets whose work is driven more by imagery than narrative, such as Wallace Stevens, Charles Simic, and Lawrence Ferlinghetti. Originally from New York City, he currently resides in England.

www.ingramcontent.com/pod-product-compliance
Lightning Source LLC
LaVergne TN
LVHW090539110826
845146LV00003B/1176

* 9 7 9 8 8 9 9 9 0 4 8 9 9 *